# WHAT DO I DO NOW?

## Building a Solid Christian Foundation

Nakia Trader

# What Do I Do Now

Building a Solid Christian Foundation

by

Nakia Trader

Copyright © 2022

ISBN: 9798847850070

Independently Published

First Edition

Unless noted otherwise, all Scripture quotations are taken from the New King James Version. Copyright © 1982 by Thomas Nelson, Inc. Used by permission. All rights reserved.
Scripture quotations marked GNT are taken from the Good News Translation. Copyright

Scripture quotations marked KJV are taken from the King James Version of the Bible.

Scripture quotations marked HCSB® are taken from the Holman Christian Standard Bible®, copyright © 1999, 2000, 2002, 2003, 2009 by Holman Bible Publishers. Used by permission. HCSB® is a federally registered trademark of Holman Bible Publishers.

*This book is dedicated to everyone who loves Jesus and wants to serve Him wholeheartedly, whose passion in life is to serve others and help them reach their full potential in Christ.*

# ACKNOWLEDGMENTS

My dear friend, Valyncia, you have inspired and encouraged me to continue to follow the Lord and always be my *real* self. Thank you for your unwavering support and belief in my God-given dreams. You have so much potential inside of you, and I hope God will give me a front-row seat to see all He is going to do through you. You are more than my friend—you're my sister. Thank you.

# PREFACE

*What do I do now?* Many new believers are faced with this question, and rightfully so. We teach and preach that we are sinners because we all have disobeyed God and receive forgiveness of sins through faith in Jesus Christ. Sharing that message is essential to the Christian life because Jesus commissioned us to *"Go into all the world and preach the gospel to every creature."* (Mark 16:15) The question is, what happens after you make a disciple and win a soul for the Kingdom of God? Do you pat the new believer on the head and say, "Go forth, my child, and continue to trust in the Lord?" Or do you take the time to instruct that person in the ways of living the Christian life according to the Word of God?

This book will not exhaust all the questions that you may have about your new life in Jesus Christ, and it is likely you will have more questions as you read this book. The purpose of this book is to give a foundation on the fundamentals of living your life in Christ. Or as my dad would like to say, "the basics." Trust me when I tell you, there have been countless times in my walk with Christ when I had to go back to the "basics" or the fundamentals. This book is not for those who have no heart to see sinners come to repentance or new believers excel in their new life as a child of God. This book is for every Christian who has ever wondered, "What do I do now?" This book is for those who wish to mentor new believers but who also need spiritual guidance in teaching people from the Bible how to become effective and God-fearing disciples of Jesus Christ. If this describes you, then let's get started!

# TABLE OF CONTENTS

# 1

## THIS IS MY STORY

"No one loves me. My dad doesn't love me. I am worthless and unworthy of love. No one will ever love me." The words flowed from my mouth. Like a waterfall, there was no end to how I was feeling inside. I was drunk and curled up inside a two-star-motel bathtub in Baltimore, MD, weighted down by ten years of accumulated sadness, loneliness, and feelings of worthlessness because of my father.

But it did not begin that way.

My father was an associate pastor at Liberty Church. People loved to come on Thursday nights and Sunday mornings to hear him preach. My father would preach so powerfully under the inspiration of the Holy Spirit that the altar was always full of people ready to give their hearts to the Lord. Knowledgeable in the Word of God, my father taught me that the most important thing for a Christian was to love and fear the Lord.

When I was 11 years old and a few weeks before school started, my four siblings and I went to a Christian summer youth camp with the other children from our church. To say the least, I was *not* excited about spending the remaining weeks of summer at a church camp. I felt miserable because I was concerned that my fellow campers would find out that I occasionally wet the bed—plus, I was just tired of going to church all the time!

I felt like my parents forced my siblings and I to go to this summer camp; therefore, I was determined to be defiant. I was smart-mouthed and sarcastic to the youth director, constantly rolling my eyes at any little thing she said and "sucking my teeth" whenever asked to do something. By the second or third day, she banished me from swimming with the other children during our free time. Instead, I was to help staff set up for the activities. I could hear laughter coming from the children—including my siblings—at the swimming pool. My heart ached at missing out on all the fun, and I determined not to continue my bad behavior. I got myself together.

Thankfully, I made it through camp without anyone finding out about my occasional bed-wetting. But more importantly, I did not finish camp that summer without meeting the most important love of my life—Jesus Christ. Up until the moment I accepted Jesus into my heart, I did not realize I was a sinner. I had often heard about John 3:16 and other oft-quoted Bible verses, but none of that mattered the night I was saved from my sin. The campers had gathered in their groups that summer night to perform dance routines, skits, and other performances for our parents, and my group was performing to Fred Hammond's "You Are the Living Word." (It's still one of my favorite songs to this day.) During the performance, I finally listened to the words after days of rehearsing to it.

After the performances, the youth pastor gave an altar call and began talking about how much God loves us and how He sent His Son to die for us. My heart felt like it was going to pound out of my chest as I listened to her, and my body began to sway uncontrollably. I tried to gain control of myself, but then I just gave up and began to cry out, "I need You, Jesus." I asked God to forgive me and accepted Jesus into my heart.

Becoming a Christian allowed my father and I to establish a relationship in which he was my mentor in Christ. He took me to Christian conventions, conferences, bookstores, and introduced me to influential Christian leaders. My father took the time to instruct me on the importance of praying and reading the Bible. From the ages of 11 to 15 were my "golden years," where I fell deeper in love with God and immersed myself in becoming the "perfect" and ideal Christian. I sought desperately to please my father to show him that I am everything he instructed me to be. He was pleased, and in my mind, I became the perfect Christian.

## The Dark Age

When I turned 16 years old, I entered what I called, "the dark age." I began to work part-time at a local mall after school and was excited to start claiming monetary independence from my parents. But as soon as I began to make money, my dad took on a new persona. He began to use hurtful words toward me, such as "worthless" and "good for nothing" because I could not afford to give him more money for gas. For years, I endured threats and insults from my Christian mentor, father, and pastor for reasons that did not make sense. I desperately wanted to please him by working hard, getting good grades, being active in church programs, being best friends with the pastor's granddaughter, giving him money, and doing whatever else he asked of me. I wanted to please him badly because he was the only person that ever took an interest in me and was my father.

The need to please him took precedence over my feelings, and I began to feel less than valued, loved, respected, worthy, happy, and a Christian. I often went to my mother about how my father was making me feel, but that only ended up making things worse on me. When my mom confronted him about it, he retaliated by picking me up late, insulting me further, calling me names, and more. Eventually, I begged my mother to stop standing up for me! Many nights I drenched my pillows with tears over the lack of understanding of how a God-fearing man could transform into someone so cruel and heartless. Losing that one person I believed I could rely on shattered my reality and broke me down to my core. I felt trapped in my mind and was unable to talk to anyone nor was I able to process those feelings. Therefore, I bottled them up. At my core, there was God. I loved Him. I loved Him so much that I fought with all my might to resist the hatred I had toward my father. I prayed more, and everything seemed to get better...for a time.

Then one night after getting off work at 9 PM, I stood outside of the mall to wait for my father to pick me up, but he didn't show up. It was pouring raining, I did not have an umbrella, and the mall doors were locked. I waited almost 2 hours in the rain for my father to pick me up. When he arrived, I was terribly upset and wanted to shout at him, "Where were you?" But I did not for fear of what he might say.

And as he drove, my dad turned and began to yell at me. He told me, "You're trying to get out of paying me gas to come pick you up every day! What a sorry excuse—" He never finished that statement. A sorry excuse for what exactly? For the rest of the ride, my father repeatedly threw insults at me and belittled me. I wasn't brave enough to speak up. I wasn't brave enough to say, "Stop! I'm not going to take this anymore!" Instead, like a punching bag, I took the jabs. My silence encouraged him to continue verbally insulting me.

I went to bed crying hysterically, telling God that I hated my dad and wished he would die. This caused me to not to trust God. I thought to myself, *If that is what godly love is like, then I do not want that love in my life.* So, knowing I shouldn't, I made the conscious decision to turn away from the Lord and live my life how I saw fit. For years, I've gone back-and-forth with God, with one foot in the world and the other in Jesus. I became the queen of backsliders. I began to party, gamble, smoke, club, drink with different crowds of people at night while also being a youth leader and active member of the church on church days.

There were times during those years when I tried to get serious about my relationship with the Lord. I left the party scene and friends by telling them, "I'm a Christian; I can't hang out with people like you." At the time, I thought it was the right approach, but what I found out was that it was hurtful. I made dozens of friends but ended up pushing them all out of my life because I did not want them to get too close to me. The moment I felt things were "good," I would sabotage it by destroying any friendship or relationship I had.

At the age of 21, I found myself staying with my best friend who lived at the pastor's house to avoid my dad. I was also drinking excessively. I drank so much that, to this day, I have no recollection of 2010. I did not know my sister had gotten pregnant or that she'd lost him in another stillborn birth. I even missed his funeral. I wasn't living home when my mom was in and out of the hospital for back-to-back heart surgeries and procedures.

In 2010, my good friend Kate and I decided that we would visit another good friend in Washington D.C. and make a girl's weekend out of it. We grabbed some wine and miniatures from the local liquor store and headed toward D.C. We felt like Thelma and Louise. The day before we were to meet our friend, we decided to have a small party in our motel room. So, we walked across the street to the liquor store for more drinks, returned to our room and blasted music. As our "party" wound down into full-blown drunkenness, I asked my friend Kate if she loved me. She said yes. Unsatisfied and in complete disbelief, I asked her why? She affirmed to me that she truly enjoyed my company and added things she loved most about our friendship. Her words made me sick to my stomach because I didn't believe what she said about me was true. In fact, I was so sickened by her words that I ran into the bathroom, slammed the door behind me, climbed into the bathtub, and cried hysterically.

Gently, Kate entered the bathroom, asking me what was wrong. I cried out, "No one loves me. My dad doesn't love me, and you certainly couldn't love me." Kate attempted to console me until I blurted out, "Why doesn't my dad love me, Kate?" She couldn't possibly have been able to answer such a question. However, she simply climbed into the bathtub with me to give me comfort, and after a while, she pulled me out and walked me to my bed to go to sleep. The rest of our trip went on smoothly, but we never spoke of that night again.

When I turned 22, my life was completely in shambles. I had no car, had no driver's license, was a college drop-out, had no money, and was in debt. At the same time, I watched my best friend go back to college, pay off credit cards, get a nice job, an apartment, and a car. I was being left behind. However, it was during my 22ⁿᵈ year of life when God began to press hard on my heart. Every moment when I was alone, God would speak to me, saying, "I'm here. Come back to Me." I wept often, knowing my lifestyle was wrong. The nudging on my heart became so strong that I heard from God even when in the middle of a nightclub. I tried my best to ignore God, knowing He wanted me to completely abandon my lifestyle and best friend and go back home to my mom and my dad.

My friend's birthday was quickly approaching, and I was on the fence, strongly contemplating turning my life back over to God. I stopped drinking and cursing. However, I wanted to show my support and celebrate my friend's birthday. On the night of my friend's birthday, a group of us women went to an expensive restaurant at the beach and then to a club in town. I was sitting outside talking to the other girls when gunshots went off in the alley next to us. I frantically ran in search of my friend so we could get to a safer place. I promised God that I would give my life back to Him if He got us out safely. I was scared but was able to retrieve my drunk friend and drove her home. That night, I had to watch over her because she was heavily intoxicated. When she eventually went to sleep, I packed my belongings determined to go home the moment I knew my friend was healthy.

The next morning, my friend was healthy enough to drive, and without asking any questions, she picked up her keys and drove me home. I didn't have to ask for a ride back nor did I ever have to explain why I was leaving after almost a year of living with her. When I got home, I unpacked my bags, got on my knees, and re-dedicated my life back to God. I asked God to forgive me and be Lord of my life for the rest of my life, and that I felt the broken me slowly being mended. In that instant, I realized that God truly loved me and that His love was nothing like my father's love.

# 2

## THIS IS MY SONG

I am completely overtaken by the second verse of the popular hymn, "Blessed Assurance."

*Perfect submission, all is at rest*
*I in my Savior am happy and blessed*
*Watching and waiting, looking above*
*Filled with His goodness, lost in His love*
*This is my story, this is my song*
*Praising my Savior all the day long*
*This is my story, this is my song*
*Praising my Savior all the day long*

One of the hardest things I had to do after I rededicated my life back to God was to learn to love myself. Now living at home with my parents, I had to once again be around my dad, and I still felt despondent toward him whenever he was in my presence. Every time I heard his voice or saw him from a distance, my natural reaction was to get as far away as possible from him. I often went to God and asked Him to help me with my feelings toward my father. When I did this, I ended up thanking Him for showing me what true love looked and felt like.

Although I was in the same situation with my father when I returned home, today, the relationship with my dad is better. I feel brand new. I finally feel the joy and indescribable peace that God's Word describes and more. I realized that no matter where I went and no matter what I did, God's love and grace remained the same, and it was enough for me. As I slowly began to talk to the Lord, He began to show me Who He was. That helped me learn to love myself. There is nothing like seeing yourself through the eyes of the Creator! *This is my song. I am free from the past, and I am free to accept the love of God through Christ Jesus.*

I read the book of Genesis, and God showed me something I had never seen before. I was able to see with my own eyes where God commanded Adam not to eat of the Tree of the Knowledge of Good and Evil. Yet, I never saw where God told Adam not to eat from the Tree of Life. That blew my mind. I was raised to just focus on the one tree God said *not* to eat from, so I had no regard to the tree they *could* eat from.

In that instant, many things opened to me. I saw the human tendency of constantly choosing wrong, but I also saw God's sovereign grace. I saw how much deeper God loved mankind before, during and after Adam's disobedience. It was in that moment when everything changed for me. I was encouraged by the Lord to dig deeper into Him. I realized I did not know how to pray, read the Bible, trust in Him, keep faith, apply Scripture to life, and much more. By the grace and mercy of God, I am excited to share what I consider to be the basics of starting a new life in Christ Jesus and having a relationship with God. These basic yet profound principles saved the little girl at summer camp, pulled the hopeless young adult out of the bathtub, and still aid in my Christian walk today. These principles are not born from my opinion, but from God's truth. As I learned them, I sought to share them. This is my opportunity to share them with you.

# 3

---

# SALVATION

*For whosoever shall call upon the name*
*of the LORD shall be saved.*
—Romans 10:13, KJV

One of the most important questions you will ever ask yourself is, "Am I saved?" At the outset, it is important that we understand our personal need for Jesus Christ to ensure that we do not miss an opportunity to introduce Christ to all. Many people have probably asked themselves this very question. In fact, it is important to ask yourself this, because as the Bible tells us, we must "work out your own salvation with fear and trembling" (Philippians 2:12). We certainly would not want to live our entire lives thinking we are saved and then stand before the Lord Jesus on Judgment Day just to hear Him say, "I never knew you; depart from Me, you who practice lawlessness!" (Matthew 7:23). What an awful day that would be for any person to hear, but especially for those who thought they lived righteously on the earth and obtained salvation! So, let us do as Scripture tells us and "work out our own salvation with fear and trembling."

*A Christian is one who maintains a right relationship with Jesus Christ and enjoys a special union with Him and which supersedes all other relationships.* Terry Pratchett stated, "If you do not know where you come from, then you don't know where you are, and if you don't know where you are, then you don't know where you're going. And if you don't know where you're going, you're probably going wrong." Far be it from me to ever presume a person is saved just because they read this book. Therefore, allow me to indulge a little on why salvation or "being saved" is significant.

To accurately answer or comprehend the question, "Am I saved?", first, we must understand what we are saved from. The word saved is a synonym for released, rescued, or delivered. In a similar way, the name of Jesus is the transliteration of the Hebrew name Joshua, which means, Savior. We can comparably say that Jesus is the Releaser, Rescuer, and Deliverer. The word savior truly suggests there is a need to be saved, that there is a threatening, deadly, or dangerous condition from which we need to be rescued. The question remains, from what are we saved from? Sin and guilt.

Many modern teachers today have watered down the Gospel message by overly emphasizing that Jesus Christ came to rescue us from our mistakes, errors, and debilitating habits so that we might have control over our own lives and have a wealthy, healthy, and prosperous future on this earth. Frankly, it is the "to live our best life now" belief as Joel Osteen has said. Although God does desire for us to live a good life while we are still on earth and certainly in the one to come, the term "good" is defined differently to God than it is for us. We will discuss this later. The watered-down Gospel that is being preached in many churches around the world tell people that they can and will have their best life now if they believe in Jesus Christ. They make strong declarations about Jesus Christ dying on the cross to save them from their mistakes in the hopes that many people will be able to identify with that message. Crazily, many people do. Because everyone makes mistakes. The issue here is that almost every human can admit to making mistakes, but not many people can admit to sinning or to being a sinner.

Do not be confused with what I am saying. Jesus can liberate and rescue you from feeling unfulfilled (because He gives you a purpose) and free you from habitually bad habits and passions (by the power of the Holy Spirit living in you giving you victory through Jesus Christ). However, these things are secondary problems to the primary issue still at work. In other words, these things are symptoms of a greater problem at hand, sin: Matthew 1:21 says, "And she will bring forth a Son, and you shall call His name Jesus, for He will *save His people from their sins*" (emphasis added).

Sin and mistake are categorically different from one another. A mistake is an action or judgment that is misguided or wrong. On the other hand, sin is an immoral act, a transgression against divine law. You cannot make a mistake without first being a sinner. You cannot make a misguided or wrong judgment without first committing an immoral act or transgression. In every facet of the word, sin reveals the depth of true human depravity that a "mistake" simply could never live up to. And Jesus came to save us from the consequences of our sin. Let's see how.

## Our Sinful Nature

In the beginning, humans were perfectly sinless beings made in the image of a holy God. We lived in close communion with our Creator and lacked nothing spiritually. Unfortunately, we sinned by disobeying God's commandment and chose to eat from one of the trees God had commanded man not to eat of. (You can find this story in the book of Genesis, chapters 1-3.) Since then, we have been in constant disobedience, rebelliousness, and defiance to God, living a life contrary to His perfect and holy will.

Perhaps you are thinking, "Wait! I did not sin or disobey God back then! That was Adam and Eve. I wasn't even in the Garden of Eden!" Yet, the infallible Word of God tells us that "all have sinned and fall short of the glory of God" (Romans 3:23). How is that possible? Well, if you have ever lied, cheated, or stolen at any time in your life, you have broken God's commandment. God said in His Word, the Bible, "You shall not steal, nor deal falsely, nor lie to one another" (Leviticus 19:11). If you think you're safe because you only broke one of the commandments, keep in mind that God's Word tells us that "whoever shall keep the whole law, and yet stumble in one point, he is guilty of all" (James 2:10). In other words, even if you have kept 99 out of 100 of God's commandments, the 1 commandment you did break makes you guilty of breaking them all.

Perhaps you may be wondering about sin you hadn't meant to commit. Is being punished for something like that fair? To me, such an example further illustrates the spiritually corrupt state we are in as humans. The true thought behind such is something like this: "I made a common mistake. I am a good person." The Bible tells us, "There is none who does good, No, not one" (Psalm 14:3 and 53:3).

The rich, young ruler learned of this lesson the hard way when he asked Jesus, "Good Teacher, what shall I do that I may inherit eternal life?" (Mark 10:17). On the surface, it appears that this rich, young man was asking a sincere question. However, when we look deeper within the context of Scripture, we see that his question was quite prideful and self-focused because He asked the Savior what *he* had to do to be saved. The rest of the story continues with Jesus responding:

> **Mark 10:18-22** — *So Jesus said to him, "Why do you call Me good? No one is good but One, that is, God. You know the commandments: 'Do not commit adultery,' 'Do not murder,' 'Do not steal,' 'Do not bear false witness,' 'Do not defraud,' 'Honor your father and your mother.'" And he answered and said to Him, "Teacher, all these things I have kept from my youth." Then Jesus, looking at him, loved him, and said to him, "One thing you lack: Go your way, sell whatever you have and give to the poor, and you will have treasure in heaven; and come, take up the cross, and follow Me." But he was sad at this word, and went away sorrowful, for he had great possessions.*

Jesus, knowing this young, rich man's heart, knew that this man had come to Him proudly with the belief that *he* was "good." Perhaps this young man was "good" by worldly standards. However, by God's standards, this man was far from good. We know this because Jesus said that "no one is good, but One, that is God." The young, rich man, deluded into thinking he was good, did not consider the fact that, firstly, despite all the good stuff he had done, he was still a sinner, and that sin would remain his problem and prevent him from inheriting eternal life. Secondly, he did not acknowledge that only Jesus (the Man he was talking to) could save him from sin since he "went away sorrowful."

It sounds like, at the conclusion of this conversation with Jesus, the young man realized that he was not "good" in the eyes of God. However, he did not (or maybe was unwilling to) let go of the mistaken belief of him being "good" in his own eyes. When we see ourselves as "good" people, we can easily justify the sin in our lives by seeing them as common mistakes. However, if there were no sin active in your life (i.e. no spiritual corruption), then not even nondeliberate mistakes would be made. You'd be perfect. You'd be "good."

God is a holy God, and there is no flaw in Him. He is perfect in all that He does and Who He is—which means His law is perfect too. God set a penalty for those who break His commandments, and that penalty is *death*. When God commanded Adam and Eve not to eat of the tree of the knowledge of good and evil, He said, "For in the day that you eat of it you shall surely die" (Genesis 2:17). Since every person has broken at least one of His commandments, we all stand guilty before the holy God, thus making death an appropriate penalty for our sin.

Now that we have established that everyone stands guilty in God's sight, how can a person be forgiven of sins? I want to be clear that having religion and having a relationship with Jesus Christ are two very different things. Often, what separates these two is found in Romans 10:9: "If you *confess with your mouth,* 'Jesus is LORD,' and *believe in your heart* that God raised him from the dead, you will be saved" (emphasis added).

## Confess with Your Mouth.

The act of using your mouth to declare words (of truth) activates your heart's response and produces life-altering reactions. Words uttered most often stem from what is in the heart of a person. Therefore, confessing with your mouth (through words) that Jesus is Lord satisfies one of the two requirements to obtain salvation.

## Believe with Your Heart

The second requirement of salvation is believing with your heart that God raised Christ Jesus from the dead. A synonym for *belief* is *faith*. God requires those who want to be saved to believe that He raised Christ Jesus from the dead and have faith that He will do the same for you and bring you to eternal life with Him.

Religious people are most often the individuals who indeed confess with their mouth that Jesus is Lord, but do not believe in their heart. These people typically attend church on Sunday and praise God. However, they live the rest of the week as the unsaved (smoking, drinking, cursing, etc.). This is contrary to those who confess with their mouth *and* believe in their heart that God raised Jesus from the dead and will also bring them to eternal life after death. These individuals will go to church on Sundays, read their Bible daily, pray, and have a desire to be like Christ. Although they will struggle daily to live for God and sometimes even fall, they will get back up and keep moving forward, having hope in their relationship with the Lord. If someone confesses something as true yet does not believe in what they are saying, then what they are doing is pointless and in vain.

If you want to be forgiven of your sins, I urge you to confess and believe according to Romans 10:9. If you feel you don't know how to frame that prayer, below is an example of a simple prayer that can change your life and eternal destiny.

*God, I admit that I have lived my life up to this point as a sinner, doing and saying anything that I desired. I am sorry. Please forgive me for all my sins. I recognize that I need someone to save me and that Someone is Jesus Christ, Your Son. I thank You for Your redemptive work on the cross where you died for my sins. I confess with my mouth that Your Son Jesus is Lord, and I believe with my whole heart that You, God, raised Jesus from the dead and will also raise me to eternal life. I ask You to come into my heart and be Lord of my life. I believe that I am now saved and am in right standing with God. Thank You, Heavenly Father. In Jesus' name, amen.*

If you prayed that prayer, allow me to congratulate you for giving your heart to our Lord and Savior, Jesus Christ! Welcome to God's family, my brother or sister in Christ!

# 4

## WHAT DOES
## THIS NEW LIFE MEAN?

I know what you must be thinking: "Okay, Kia, I am now saved, but what do I do now?" Well, before knowing what your next step is, you should ask yourself, "What does this new life mean?" Simply put, it means *everything* you could ever imagine.

A.W. Tozer said, "The crucified life is a life absolutely committed to following Christ Jesus. To be more like Him. To think like Him. To act like Him. To love like Him. The whole essence of spiritual perfection has everything to do with Jesus Christ. Not with rules and regulations. Not with how we dress or what we do or do not do. We are not to look like each other; rather, we are to look like Christ. We can get all caught up in nuances of religion and miss the glorious joy of following after Christ. Whatever hinders us in our journey must be dealt a deathblow."

In Luke 8, we find the story of a woman named Mary Magdalene who was considered by those in her town to be among the most unstable of women. She often suffered episodes of violent epilepsy and insanity that catapulted her into a realm of seeming hopelessness. Mary's reputation was tarnished, as she was simply left to deal with her hopeless condition on her own. One day, Jesus and His disciples were in her town, healing the sick and preaching the Kingdom of God. Jesus spotted Mary and approached her because He was *moved with compassion.* When He met Mary, He knew instantly that this woman needed His help. He was the only One who saw what was really going on with Mary. Jesus cast seven demons (or devils) out of Mary—demons that were stealing her sanity and weakening her body.

After Jesus touched her, Mary was made whole. Her mind was restored, and her epileptic condition disappeared. Mary worshipped Jesus and decided to join His followers by becoming His disciple. Mary decided to devote her entire life to following and being taught by Jesus. Undoubtedly, Mary learned about the Kingdom of God and heard the parables of the sower (Matthew 13) and of the mustard seed of faith (Mark 4). She was present when Jesus blessed and fed both the 4,000 and the 5,000 men. Mary is mentioned at least ten times in the Gospels and is conveyed as having a deep love for Christ Jesus. The Bible tells us that "Mary Magdalene and Mary the mother of Joses observed where He was laid" (Mark 15:47).

What I love about Mary Magdalene is that, when she met Jesus, her life was instantly changed and her love for Him was apparent even after He was crucified. She was the first one to see the resurrected Christ and even shared the good news with His disciples. Although only a few of Jesus' disciples believed Mary's report, Mary knew in her heart that her Beloved Savior had risen!

Mary loved Jesus, the One Who gave her a new chance at life. And how did she respond? She followed Him, learned from Him, and became like Him day by day. Mary is a perfect example of a life changed by Christ. My brother once shared this profound verse of Scripture with me: "Therefore I say to you, her sins, which are many, are forgiven, for she loved much. But to whom little is forgiven, the same loves little" (Luke 7:47). Those who realize that Christ has forgiven them for many sins will in turn love greatly and be driven by that love to serve Him.

Growing up, my father repeatedly told me, "When someone truly meets Jesus, their life will never be the same." Truer words have never been spoken. When I met Jesus, my life did not mystically fall into place and neither did all my problems immediately disappear. However, my life was never the same again. If you have decided to become a Christian, you know full well why a person's life is forever changed by Jesus Christ.

In all that life has handed me, God remains right by my side. Through the darkest valleys and on the highest mountain-tops, Christ is there walking with me, teaching me His Word, and helping me grow to resemble Him. Even now, I make it my priority in life to continue to grow to resemble Jesus. I still fall, sin, and sometimes I miss the mark by miles, but Christ pursues me with His unfailing love and corrects me when I am wrong. What a tremendous love to give someone who is un-worthy! What a blessed hope we have in Jesus!

A.W. Tozer said it best in his book, *The Crucified Life*, "Living the crucified life is a journey not for the faint at heart. The journey is rough and filled with dangers and difficulties, and it does not end until we see Christ. Yet though the journey may be difficult, the result of seeing Christ face-to-face is worth it all."

The Bible records the transformation of many lives through the power of Jesus Christ. Take, for instance, Paul. Paul, who was named Saul at the time, "made havoc of the church, entering every house, and dragging off men and women, committing them to prison" (Acts 8:3). Saul was a religious leader and prominent speaker who heavily persecuted the church and consented to the death of Stephen for preaching in the name of Jesus. I could imagine if I met someone like Paul today, it would be difficult for me to see how God could change the heart of such a Christ-hating man. But God did just that for Paul!

On the road to Damascus, Christ appeared to Saul who was on a mission to remove all those who "were of the Way (Jesus)" and "bring them bound to Jerusalem" (Acts 9:2). On that road to Damascus, Saul's life was forever changed when he came face to face with Christ! After some time, Saul emerged as Paul and began to boldly proclaim the name of Jesus Christ to both the Jews and the Gentiles. Paul became a powerful vessel used to advance the Kingdom of God and spread the Good News throughout the world. Paul and Mary are just two examples of people whom the world counted as helpless wretches and yet God saved and used both for His purposes.

Imagine that you are the black sheep of your family. You are the one who breaks the laws and will not stop doing so. Despite the best efforts of your family to reform you, you turn them away and become fully engrossed in the world of gang affiliations and drugs. Eventually, you end up being caught for robbery. Your friends and family have both deserted you, and you begin to feel remorseful. In court, the charges brought against you are significant enough to put you away in jail for years…unless you can give back the money you stole. With no way of paying back the money, you are resigned to the fact that you are going to jail—until a Man you've never met comes in and hands the judge the amount required for your freedom.

The judge accepts the money and says to you, "You can go. Your debt has been paid. Go, and stay out of trouble."

Filled with tremendous gratitude, you approach the Man who paid your debt and ask Him, "What can I do to show You how thankful I am that You paid my debt?"

The Man replies, "Follow Me, and I will change your life." And you do!

Like Mary Magdalene, by now you should understand that Jesus Christ has saved and forgiven you for so much. But what does that all mean? The Bible tells us that "if anyone is in Christ, he is a new creation (or creature), old things have passed away; behold, all things have become new" (2 Corinthians 5:17). When you believed and confessed Christ, instantly you become a new creature. Essentially, your sins have been forgiven and the blood of Christ has been applied to your life. In fact, you could say an exchange took place. Christ Jesus took our sin, and in return, He gave us His new life. Praise His holy name!

You are now a child of God. You are now free from the eternal consequences of sin and completely free to live your brand-new life for God. Remember, those who realize that Christ has forgiven them for many sins will in turn love greatly and be driven by that love to serve Him. I can say with confidence that when God sees you, He sees Christ's blood covering you. He sees that indestructible blood that was shed on Calvary to forgive your sins. You are a new creature.

## Perfection

This new life in Christ does not mean that we are to be perfect in all that we do, in all that we say or all that we think. Yes, I know, the world expects Christians to be perfect (flawless) simply because we are, well, Christians. No other religion or faith expects their followers to be perfect, but when it comes to Christianity, things become different. It's an interesting phenomenon, but I digress.

I would be remiss if I did not share this one monumental fact that I have struggled with in my personal journey in Christ: we are not perfect, but God does expect perfection. Now, for those who are familiar with the verse that says, *"Therefore you shall be perfect, just as your Father in heaven is perfect"* (Matthew 5:48, NKJV), you are likely wondering why Jesus says to be perfect and Nakia says we can never be perfect. Allow me to elaborate on this seeming contradiction.

"You shall be perfect, just as your Father in heaven is perfect." Those words that Jesus spoke are straight forward. There is no riddle to be solved or interpretation to be made with His statement. He did not say, "Try to be perfect." He meant exactly what He said. However, the context of this verse gives us a clearer meaning to Jesus' statement. Jesus did not expect the multitude of people that were listening to Him that day on the mountain to run out and be perfect. He certainly does not expect us to read that verse and be perfect. It would be impossible to do so. Simply put, if we could be perfect, we would not have needed Christ in the first place. Furthermore, being "new creatures" in Christ does not mean we are going to be perfect. We will still sin and still make mistakes. The difference is that we have the Holy Spirit to help us. In other words, we have the One Who is perfect living inside of us to perfect us—that is to bring us to maturity in Christ.

What Jesus was saying on the mountain that day was to illustrate God's holy standard. God is a holy and perfect God. His standard cannot be less than His character because He is perfect (flawless) and exceedingly righteous. Jesus told the multitude and us today that since the law was first given to Moses, God has stated that He expects perfection from His people. God's law and Jesus' statement were intended to make one point and yield one fruitful response to those who listened and heeded: to make us realize that there is a very high standard of living in the eyes of God and there is no way to achieve it on our own.

Matthew 5:48 was meant to be taken as a brick wall and meant to astonish us and stop us in our tracks in thinking wrongly about our righteousness. This impossible demand was meant to solicit questions such as:

- How can I ever be perfect?
- How can I be saved?
- How can I achieve such an impossible standard?

The answer is, was, and will always be Jesus Christ. Pastor John MacArthur writes, "The marvelous truth of the Gospel is that Christ has met this standard on our behalf and our response should be to believe in Christ." Through Jesus, we have been imputed righteousness (perfection) by grace through faith. So now, for those who have decided to believe and follow Christ Jesus, God sees perfection—the perfection of Jesus given in salvation. Although we will continue to make

mistakes and sin, because of Christ, we are perfect in our jus-
tification before God.

# 5

## HOW CAN I BE
## SURE I AM SAVED?

My good friend and ministry partner received Christ in 2016. Up until then, she and I often had conversations concerning spiritual matters, and she frequently expressed interest in going to church. One Sunday, she finally attended with me and gave her life to Jesus Christ a few days later.

In 2017, I asked her to join me in beginning a ministry that focused on connecting Christians around the world for strength, encouragement, and fellowship. Since that beginning, we have faced countless mountaintop blessings from God as well as seemingly endless months in the valley of persecution. During one of those humble times in the valley, she shared with me that there was a brief time after she accepted Christ when she was not sure she was saved. I began to feel guilty because I had not taken the time to address the importance of identifying who we are in Christ and being certain that she understood this truth.

My friend has since asked me numerous questions that focus on what being a Christian look like in the eyes of God. Most, if not all, of her questions are one's I've asked myself at one time. One example is, "Am I saved?" Have you ever doubted your salvation after you accepted Jesus Christ? If so, you are one among many Christians who have asked the very same question!

I promise you, if you truly asked Christ to forgive you of your sins, accepted His atonement for your sins, and asked Him to be Lord of your life, I can say with tremendous confidence that you are saved. Yet, as humans, we sometimes still have reservations about these things. Allow me to address some of the most common concerns and misconceptions among new and mature believers.

## You Don't *Feel* Saved

*Emotions rise up and then move out, wanting us to follow them. When I feel that, I know I need to take action!* —Joyce Meyer

Perhaps you have doubted your salvation because you do not *feel* anything is happening to, in, for, or through you. Salvation is not based on feelings. In fact, most mature Christians never discuss *feeling* saved. They just *know* they are saved without having to think about it. Why? Mature Christians know that feelings change and, because they change, they are not a dependable source of truth; only the Bible is! God cannot lie. That means His Word is the truth.

Salvation is a *spiritual* matter, as it affects not the physical but the spiritual condition of every human that accepts Christ. When Adam and Eve disobeyed God, the consequence (as previously discussed) was death. Death is not only a physical consequence of sin but also the death of the spiritual man. This means that every human since Adam has been born spiritually dead (separated eternally from God). God's will is that no man should be separated from Him. Therefore, He made a promise in Genesis to reconcile humans back to Himself so we would not be eternally separated from Him.

## Doubt

Unfortunately, doubting is common among Christians. The devil, the source of those doubts, takes great pleasure in bringing various doubts to our minds. The devil's objective is to cause Christians to doubt whether they are saved or good enough. He hopes that such doubts will cause the believer to become stagnant and ineffective in their walk with the Lord. Billy Graham said, "When we doubt our salvation, we doubt God's Word; and when we doubt God's Word, we are powerless and ineffective tools for Christ."

The harsh reality is that none of us are good enough to be called Christians. We never were. However, because God loves us, He sent Jesus Christ to die for us. And now that He has risen from the grave, we can have eternal life by *grace* through faith in His Son. The only way to keep from doubting is to believe. *To believe* essentially means *to have faith*. "Faith is the substance of things hoped for, the evidence of things not seen" (Hebrews 11:1).

## The Bible Tells You So

The Bible tells us, "For by grace you have been saved through faith, and that not of yourselves; it is the gift of God"

(Ephesians 2:8). We are saved by the grace of God and cannot earn salvation by any performance. Grace is God's unmerited favor toward men because He loves us. His love cannot be earned, but we can, by faith, know we are saved. Believing we are saved and that we have eternal life will free us to live fully for the Lord Jesus Christ.

Other key verses pertaining to salvation are found in 1 John 5. In 1 John 5:1, John reminds the believer: "Whoever believes that Jesus is the Christ is born of God." In the following verses, John lays out a key point to every believer about what it means to be born of God and how to combat the doubts that often flood our mind: "For whatever is born of God overcomes the world. And this is the victory that has overcome the world—our faith" (1 John 5:4). Faith is fear's worst enemy, and it has an unstoppable power to destroy doubts, worries, and "every high thing that exalts itself against the knowledge of God, bringing every thought into captivity to the obedience of Christ" (2 Corinthians 10:5).

The Apostle John walked closely with Jesus Himself and, as the Bible describes, John was the one *"whom Jesus loved"* (John 13:23). Undoubtedly, John received in-depth discipleship from the Teacher and knew Him intimately. I would say that John is qualified to instruct us regarding the truth. "These things I have written to you who believe in the name of the Son of God, that you may know that you have eternal life, and that you may continue to believe in the name of the Son of God" (1 John 5:13).

Eternal life does not begin when we die, but it exists within us right now because we have Him Who is eternal inside of us—the Holy Spirit.

# The Holy Spirit

The Holy Spirit is one of three distinct persons of the Holy Trinity. He is the Spirit of the Living God Who is in Jesus and now lives in the heart of every believer. The Holy Spirit is the key component in a Christian's life and a powerful indication of salvation. The Holy Spirit is vital in the life of every Christian. In fact, we could not be called children of God if we did not possess His Holy Spirit. The Bible tells us that we are saved because we have the promised Holy Spirit living inside of us: "In Him you also trusted, after you heard the word of truth, the gospel of your salvation; in whom also, having believed, you were sealed with the Holy Spirit of promise" (Ephesians 1:13). The Holy Spirit is a seal that a believer is saved and possesses an inheritance of eternal life with God. "Who [*the Holy Spirit*] is the guarantee of our inheritance until the redemption of the purchased possession, to the praise of His glory" (Ephesians 1:14, emphasis added).

God knows that, while our sins are forgiven and we have been washed by the blood of Jesus Christ, we need help if we are to be like His Son. Therefore, before His ascension, Jesus promised to send His disciples the Helper and "comforter, which is the Holy Ghost [*or Spirit*], whom the Father will send in my name." (John 14:26, KJV, emphasis added)

The Greek word for comforter is **paraclete**, which means "one who consoles or comforts, one who encourages or uplifts; hence refreshes, and/or one who intercedes on our behalf as an advocate in court." In other Bible translations, they use *Counselor* to describe the role of the Holy Spirit in the life of the Christian. Counselor means, in the Greek translation, "One who is called alongside." In Jesus' absence, the Holy

Spirit is called to or sent alongside the Christian as a comforter, refresher, teacher, and advocate. And like any good disciple (or student), we are to listen, learn, and be obedient to the Holy Spirit's voice, because it is the voice of God Himself!

Trust me when I tell you that there is absolutely no way I would be able to take one step in this walk with the Lord if it weren't for the Holy Spirit. For me, the Holy Spirit has always been that Person Who was separate from God and Jesus. However, after I re-dedicated my life back to the Lord, I discovered that the Holy Spirit is Who I need most to help me live freely in God. The Holy Spirit is the One Who can teach me, remind me, correct me, comfort me, walk alongside of me, and do much more. He is no longer a distant Person to me; He is the very reason why I am breathing right now.

As Christians, the Holy Spirit has come to "guide you into all truth; for He will not speak on His own authority, but whatever He hears He will speak; and He will tell you things to come. He will glorify Me, for He will take of what is Mine and declare it to you" (John 16:13-14).

With the powerful workings of the Holy Spirit, He will lead and guide all true believers in the ways of God. Being led by the Holy Spirit will manifest in many ways that will cause us to produce the God-desired fruit, better known as the fruit of the Spirit. In Galatians 5:22-23, Paul tells us that these manifestations the Spirit produces in a true Christian's life are undeniable because "you will know them [*Christians*] by their fruit" (Matthew 7:16, emphasis added). And we also see that "the fruit of the Spirit is love, joy, peace, longsuffering, kindness, goodness, faithfulness, gentleness, self-control. Against such there is no law" (Galatians 5:22-23).

To leave the life of doubting our salvation, we must hold fast to the promises of God. We have been saved (by the blood of Christ), sanctified (for God) and filled with the Holy Spirit because we believe in Jesus Christ.

# 6

---

## WHAT DO I DO NOW?

"**I** have decided to follow Jesus, so what do I do now?" Believe it or not, this is a very common question that many have but some are afraid to ask. I was blessed to have a foundation in the Lord and someone to explain many of the most complicated Christian topics, such as faith, love, forgiveness, and so on. However, others were not necessarily blessed to have my Christian background or have someone to answer their questions. The purpose of this chapter is to answer some of the most commonly asked questions for new believers in Christ. I am hoping this will provide guidance, encouragement, and hope to all who seek an answer to the question: "What do I do now?"

### Find a Faith-Based Church

Being rooted in a church is important for the growth of every Christian.

> **Hebrews 10:24-25** — *And let us consider one another in order to stir up love and good works, not forsaking the assembling of ourselves together, as is the*

*manner of some, but exhorting one another, and so*
*much the more as you see the Day approaching.*

## Why Should I Go to Church?

For every Christian, there will be days when you need encouragement and prayer from another Christian. Therefore, assembling with other like-minded Christians at least once a week will provide the fellowship needed to get you through difficult times as we live in this sinful world.

Admittedly, growing up, I didn't think I needed to be in church as often as my parents made me go. So, when I became an adult, I stopped attending church regularly. But after rededicating myself to God, I understood that assembling with other Christ-followers was essential to my Christian walk. I was able to glean from their experiences as a Christian, comprehend deeper meanings surrounding Bible verses and stories, be encouraged, learn to worship and praise, and so much more. As I attended church regularly, I began to see my life bear the fruit of righteousness.

The Bible gives accounts of first-century Christians often meeting in houses to fellowship with one another. Fellowship is defined as a group of people meeting to pursue a shared interest or aim being equally yoked together in fellowship with other Christians will provide you with a deeper understanding of Jesus Christ. Acts records several passages of Scripture that show the early first-century Christians fellowshipping with each other. Acts 20:7 is just one example.

*Now on the first day of the week, when the disciples*
*came together to break bread, Paul, ready to depart the*

*next day, spoke to them and continued his message until midnight.*

One of the most powerful assemblies occurred in Acts 2:1-3, when the Holy Spirit came.

> *When the Day of Pentecost had fully come, they were all with one accord in one place. And suddenly there came a sound from heaven, as of a rushing mighty wind, and it filled the whole house where they were sitting. Then there appeared to them divided tongues, as of fire, and one sat upon each of them.*

Amazing things are guaranteed to happen when Christians come together to worship, praise, pray, and discuss their faith in Jesus Christ. This is because the Lord Jesus promised, "For where two or three are gathered together in My name, I am there in the midst of them" (Matthew 18:20).

Growing up in the church, my eyes have been opened to many opportunities, revelations, relationships, experiences, and so forth. I would not trade them for the world. I have seen the presence of the Lord fall on the congregation to the point that no formal preaching was necessary. I have seen adults and children set free from demonic influences, the lame walk, and people healed from various diseases. I have even seen an angel wrap his arms around the senior pastor as she gave a sermon one Sunday. Not every Sunday or weekly gathering would be as profound as I have just described. However, I can promise you that you would not want to miss and be left out of the experience. Do not permit yourself to miss out while you watch everyone who goes to church receive the inspiration, motivation, Word of God, guidance, and the direction they need.

## Be Baptized

> **Matthew 28:19-20** – *Go therefore and make disciples of all the nations, baptizing them in the name of the Father and of the Son and of the Holy Spirit, teaching them to observe all things that I have commanded you; and lo, I am with you always, even to the end of the age. Amen.*

As Christians, we are to be in fellowship with the other members of the body of Christ. Like our brothers and sisters in Christ, we are to teach those who come to Christ to *observe all things* that Jesus commanded us in His Word. However, believers cannot be taught effectively until they are baptized in the Holy Spirit.

## What Is Baptism?

Baptism is one of two ordinances given by Jesus Christ to His church. Baptism is a public profession of faith and of discipleship with Christ. It is a symbolic representation of the death, burial, and resurrection of Christ. When a believer makes a public profession of faith in Christ by being baptized, the submersion under water pictures death to our old selves (to sin). Being under water pictures being purified and cleansed by the power of the Holy Spirit following salvation. Coming up out of the water symbolizes being resurrected to a new life in Christ.

**Romans 6:4** – *Therefore, we were buried with Him through baptism into death, that just as Christ was raised from the dead by the glory of the Father, even so we also should walk in newness of life.*

When we ask Christ into our hearts, the Holy Spirit is deposited in us. When we are baptized, we deposit ourselves in the Holy Spirit. Almost always, the sequence that occurs for a new believer is:

1. Salvation
2. Baptism
3. Teaching

As an example, in Acts 2:41, we see 3,000 people receive salvation and immediately get baptized. After He was saved, the Apostle Paul was baptized instantly. In Acts 16:14-15, we see that a woman named Lydia received salvation after hearing Paul speak, and she and her household were immediately baptized.

## Do I Make a Promise When I Am Baptized?

When believers are baptized, they make a promise to God to fear Him and keep His commandments.

**Ecclesiastes 12:13, KJV** – *Let us hear the conclusion of the whole matter: Fear God and keep his commandments: for this is the whole duty of man.*

Baptism is the believer's obedience to Jesus after salvation because it is an outward testimony of the inward change in a believer's life—or to put it more simply, an outward expression of the inward confession. Therefore, look for an opportunity in your church to be baptized as soon as you are permitted.

## Read the Bible

One of the most important things that every Christian should do is read the Bible. As previously mentioned, whether you are a new believer or a mature believer, reading the Bible is crucial. I have already mentioned my struggle when I did not read the Bible and how it greatly impacted my walk with God. So, from the bottom of my heart, I implore you to set a time daily to read and study the Bible.

> **2 Timothy 2:15, KJV** – *Study to show thyself approved unto God, a workman that needeth not to be ashamed, rightly dividing the word of truth.*

When you choose a version of the Bible to read, be aware that some versions omit or change verses that are critical to correct Bible doctrine. The following versions are my personal favorites: The New King James Version, the King James Version, and the Amplified Bible.

## Why Do I Need to Read the Bible?

Just like we need food for *physical* nourishment and strength, the believer needs the Bible for *spiritual* guidance, strength, and nourishment. We must "be fed" with the Word of God and receive divine sustenance so that we can grow in spiritual maturity. For years, I have seen Christians starve themselves by not feeding their spirits on the Word of God. Their lives consist of going to work, eating, watching television, and going to bed. There is rarely time dedicated to reading the Bible, and on the day when they feel discouraged, defeated, overwhelmed, persecuted, angry, and so on, they lack the divine sustenance that nourishes our lives.

## How Should I Begin Reading My Bible?

In everything I do, I go to God first before I go to anyone else—and there could not be a more perfect time to go to Him than before you begin reading the Bible. I believe it is key to start by praying. I ask God to reveal His Word to me by leading and guiding me through the help of the Holy Spirit. I also thank Him for the honor and privilege of reading His Holy Word and declare that, whatever He chooses to reveal to me in the Bible, I will be sure to speak it, meditate on it, stand on it, and trust Him.

> *Ephesians 1:17-18 – That the God of our Lord Jesus Christ, the Father of glory, may give to you the spirit of wisdom and revelation in the knowledge of Him, the eyes of your understanding being enlightened; that you may know what the hope of His calling is, what are the riches of the glory of His inheritance in the saints.*

## What Do I Read First in the Bible?

As you draw closer to God, He will speak to your heart regarding where He wants you to read and focus your attention. He will deposit in your spirit the topics, words, verses, and chapters that He wants you to read. I encourage you to listen to the leading of that still small voice. If you aren't sure the voice you hear is God speaking to you, remember that Satan will never tell you to do something that will feed your spirit. So, get quiet and listen for God's voice. The more you obey, the easier it will become to recognize His voice.

If you don't believe you have heard His voice and want to get started, you have many options for reading God's Word.

### Devotionals

Using devotional books is a good way to ensure you read the Bible daily. Such materials have proven to be an effective way to help Christians gain a deeper understanding of a passage of Scripture.

### Bible Concordance

A Bible concordance is a listing of words and phrases found in the Holy Bible. It shows where terms occur throughout all books of Scripture. The concordance contains cross-references for verses to make it easy to understand the meaning of terms and the context in which those words are used.

### My Personal Suggestion

The Bible is a big deal. I mean, reading the Bible is a massive undertaking whether you are a new Christian or not. My suggestion in deciding on where to begin when reading the Bible is to turn to one of the "beginnings." In other words, begin with either the first book of the Old Testament (Genesis) or the first book of the New Testament (Matthew).

If you are a new believer, I think it is best to begin with the Gospels (Matthew, Mark, Luke, and John) and then continue through the rest of the New Testament. I suggest this because the Gospels tell of the life of Jesus—Who He is and what He has done.

As a preview, Acts shares with us the power of the Holy Spirit at work in first-century Christians and the power that dwells within you right now. Some suggest that you begin with the book of John then move forward through the New Testament. I believe this reasoning is because John shows Jesus Christ as the Son of God. The Gospel of John provides a clearer understanding and richer text than the other Gospels of the divinity of Christ. However, no matter where you decide to begin, I suggest you begin in the Gospels and learn of the life of our Beloved Savior.

For the Christian who has been saved for a while, I always find comfort in going back to "my roots," and by that, I mean the book of Genesis. The creation of the world, the consequences of sin, and faith-testing situations are all found in that marvelous book, but I might be biased. Just know that regardless of where you choose to begin, God will be there with you.

## How Much Should I Read?

Many Christians struggle in determining how much of God's Word they should be reading, as if there is a quota that needs to be filled. I once heard a preacher say, "There are microwave Christians and there are crockpot Christians. The microwave Christians want their information and understanding as quickly as possible. On the other hand, the crockpot Christians understand that the Word of God is something that should not be quickly cooked but simmered and marinated because the food is more savory than the microwave experience." It is imperative to set a time daily to read and study the Bible. However, quantity should not be the focus or goal when reading or studying the Bible.

Read for quality, not quantity. We must focus on taking in the richness of what we read in God's Word instead of skimming through the Bible. We must understand that it is better to be able to say, "I read one verse and learned to apply it to my life," than to say, "I read five chapters and have no idea what to make of it." Take your time when reading the divinely inspired Word of God.

## How Do I Understand What I Am Reading?

The Bible tells us in 2 Timothy 2:7, "The Lord give you understanding in all things." I remember my friend asking me this question while I was at work one evening, and I contemplated the best way to answer. The best way to understand *what* you are reading is to understand *why* you are reading. We read the Bible because the Bible was given to *guide us* (in behavior, feelings, thoughts, etc.) so that we will reflect God. Understanding that God's Word was given to guide us helps us look at each verse in the scope of Him guiding us in this world.

To understand what you are reading in the Bible, you must *study* the Bible. It is the Lord's great pleasure to have us understand what we are reading in His word. But studying is not a mental exercise like what we do when studying for an exam; instead, it is an exercise of the heart that must be applied when reading. In other words, studying is more than just using your mind to comprehend material. It is using your heart to understand the mysteries of God revealed through the Bible.

It doesn't matter who the smartest person on this planet is; at best, our minds are limited in understanding and comprehension. This is especially true as we attempt to understand God. Essentially, we are attempting to understand an infinite God with a finite mind. Despite that limitation, God made us truly unique! When He created us, God gave us the capacity to understand Him through our hearts. The heart is figuratively expandable in many ways. It can shrink (when we lose trust in someone or something) or it can expand and grow (as we trust and love). So, the fact that God places understanding within our hearts should be the key we utilize while studying to understand the Bible.

God does not expect us to follow the opinion of others. His desire is that we personally discover Him through His Word. Therefore, when we *continually* apply our hearts in studying the Bible by putting our mind, will, and emotions to rest, we will understand what we are reading in the Bible, because God "is a rewarder of those who diligently seek Him" (Hebrews 11:6), and God will not allow us to pursue the truth of God without His help. (Finding His truth without His help would be impossible.) God provides this help through the Holy Spirit.

> **John 16:13, KJV** – *Howbeit when he, the Spirit of truth, is come, he will guide you into all truth: for he shall not speak of himself; but whatsoever he shall hear, that shall he speak: and he will shew you things to come.*

With the Holy Spirit's help, when we study the Bible by applying our hearts to understanding, we will receive insight regarding what we are reading.

## How Do I Study the Bible?

This question is one of the most searched topics of interest for Christians. Christians often desire to read the Word of God but have no idea how they ought to study the Bible. Below is an acronym using the word SOAP that will offer some guidance in this area.

- **(S)cripture** – Select somewhere between three and ten verses of Scripture and read them through three times.

- **(O)bservation** – Write down some observations about the verses. For example, look for repeated words, determine the central point of the passage, look up the meaning of words you don't know, and check the meanings of any names in a Bible dictionary.

- **(A)pplication** – This is a vital step. Ask yourself how you can apply to your life what you've read or observed. Meditate on the message the verses have for you. Ask yourself what God is trying to convey to you through His Word.

- **(P)rayer** – You can't pray enough! Ask for leading from the Spirit to live what God has revealed to you.

I have always found it useful to keep a notebook to write down my thoughts about verses, names, locations, cross-references, and so forth so that I can refer to it later. I have personally found many different techniques useful when studying the Bible, such as writing scriptures on notebook paper, using highlighters to emphasize certain verses, using index cards to memorize and recall verses, and more. The important techniques to utilize are the ones that work best for your personal life. Allow SOAP to become a guideline in helping you learn to study the Bible.

## Prayer

As children of God, we have been given access to God's presence at any time through prayer. Because of Jesus Christ, we have the right to go directly to God and share with Him our thoughts, feelings, desires, fears, petitions, and requests. In its simplest form, prayer is communication (talking) with God.

I know that in the earlier stages of my Christian walk, I did not comprehend even the simplest definition of prayer. I remember thinking, "All I have to do is talk to God like I am talking to my friends; well, that'll be easy!" I quickly learned that was not the case at all. If you want to know what prayer is, you must look in the Scripture to fully understand the concept of praying in Christian faith.

I've concluded that, for me, praying is not like talking to my friends. When I was first saved, I approached God something like this: "Hey, God, I need You to help me because my friends are getting on my nerves, and I am getting quite fed up with them. I'm trying to do what You want me to do, but I'm about to go off on them. I can't take it anymore!" While I believe it is important to be honest with God about your feelings in prayer and equally important to remember that God is your friend, I believe it is more important to remember that God is also holy and there is no one like Him! Praying is more than talking to your friend; it is an act of worship and a time of confession and petition. Be sure not to leave out those aspects of prayer.

## Should I Be Praying Daily?

I have never met a true Christian who did not pray, and God's Word says that we must "pray without ceasing" (1

Thessalonians 5:17). Praying should be a daily endeavor because we cannot do God's will each day if we do not give ourselves the opportunity for Him to tell us His plans in prayer. Praying should be a daily practice for every Christian who desires to live in the fullness of God.

## Why Should I Pray?

We should pray daily because, if we do not, we will lack the power, insight, and spiritual guidance that we need in our lives. If we do not come before Him to commune with Him, then we cut ourselves off from His glory.

Think about it this way: If you have a friend who you don't call or communicate with in any way, do you believe your friendship will grow? I can tell you that it will not. In fact, that relationship will not only become stagnant but also will be the opposite of its original intent. For Christians, prayer is crucial to learning about and living the life God has designed you to live.

## Prayer Keeps Us Connected

Prayer is communication with God, how we receive information, power, and strength. Communication is an exchange of ideas and information to evoke understanding. Prayer is an intimate discussion and the perfect means for you to speak with God about your day and feelings, and it also gives God the opportunity to speak with you as well.

I liken prayer to a lamp and an electrical socket. To stay connected to God (the Light), we must plug our lamp cord into the electrical socket to receive power. Praying in conjunction with reading the Bible is the only means through which God allows us to connect with Him.

## Prayer Is How We Confess Sin

Let's be honest. Even the "greatest" Christian still sins, and perhaps sins daily. I know I do. And I, like Paul, consider myself to be "less than the least of all the saints" (Ephesians 3:8). Since "all have sinned and fall short of the glory of God," it is important to communicate with God and confess our sins so we can live a full and rich life in God. Prayer is the only way to ask God to forgive us of our sins through repentance and to seek His help in overcoming the sins that so easily beset us. The Bible tells us that "If we confess our sins, He is faithful and just to forgive us our sins and to cleanse us from all unrighteousness" (1 John 1:9). Thus, as we go before our Heavenly Father daily in prayer and confess all known sin in our lives, we will keep ourselves pure and better able to avoid sin's devastating effects.

## Prayer Is How We Praise and Worship

Christians are commanded to "give thanks to the Lord, for he is good; for his steadfast love endures forever!" (1 Chronicles 16:34). Prayer affords believers the opportunity to offer praise, worship, and thanksgiving to God for the many blessings He gives. We ought not go a day without expressing to God how thankful we are for all He has done for us! The book of Psalms provides marvelous expressions of praise and exaltation to God. Here are a few good examples:

**Psalm 8:1** – *O Lord, our Lord, How excellent is Your name in all the earth, Who have set Your glory above the heavens.*

**Psalm 9:1** – *I will praise You, O LORD, with my whole heart; I will tell of all Your marvelous works.*

The Psalms almost always begin with praise for our God. Beginning your prayer with praise and worship of God is the appropriate way of praying. God's very name is to be sanctified (set apart) as holy. God's name is not like any other name; His name is great! "Great is the Lord, and greatly to be praised" (Psalm 48:1). His steadfast love and abundant provision for our lives warrant acknowledgment, admiration, and acclamation from all who trust in God.

## Prayer Gives Us Access to God's Power

Many Christians do not realize the insurmountable power that prayer holds. It is so powerful that Paul writes in Ephesians a list of the pieces of God's infallible armor, but gives us two weapons to use, the sword of the Spirit (which is the Word of God) and prayer. Every Christian must pray because God has given us prayer to bring heaven to the earth. This is *only* accomplished by praying. We will rarely, if ever, see God's Kingdom come and His will be done on the earth if we do not pray.

The Bible teaches us about who Jesus is and about His will and plan for us. God has given us everything we need to become the believers He created us to be. However, because He gave us a freewill, He cannot and will not act upon the earth until we pray (or ask Him to do so).

In Genesis 1:26, God said, "Let us make man in our image, after our likeness: and let them have dominion." Dr. Myles Munroe explains it this way: "God is only as sovereign as His Word. He will never violate His Word. And God is limited by His Word." In other words, God gave us dominion (control) over the things of the earth because we are created in His image. He expects us to have dominion over the earth as He has dominion over all things. And He reveals to us how He rules and reigns over His creation through the Bible. We must seek the Lord and study the Bible to learn what God's will is on the earth and use His Word in prayer. This is called praying in the Spirit.

To give you an example, the Word of God declares, "But my God shall supply all your need according to his riches in glory by Christ Jesus" (Philippians 4:19, KJV). In this scripture, we understand that God will take care of our needs because He has created all things and because all things belong to Him. So, when we approach God in prayer, we can approach Him confidently by saying, "Heavenly Father, You know the situation I am in, 'and are acquainted with all my ways.' I need You to please intervene on my behalf because Your Word declares that You, 'my God shall supply all your need according to his riches in glory by Christ Jesus.' I believe that Your Word is true, and I know You will supply all my need. I love You, and I thank You for Your promises. In Jesus' name I pray. Amen."

## How Do I Pray?

This is one of the most frequently asked questions among Christians. I have personally struggled with this in my own walk with the Lord. In Matthew 6:9-13, however, Jesus tells us how we ought to pray

> *In this manner, therefore, pray: Our Father in heaven, Hallowed be Your name, Your kingdom come. Your will be done on earth as it is in heaven. Give us this day our daily bread. And forgive us our debts, as we forgive our debtors. And do not lead us into temptation but deliver us from the evil one.*

Let's consider what we can learn from this passage of scripture:

1. Pray to your Heavenly Father (God) in a way that honors Him as holy. God is not like mankind; He is perfect and righteous, and He should be hallowed (honored) as such. He deserves all praise. As you begin to praise God, you will find yourself ushered into the presence of the Lord and your mind will be set on the things of God. You will begin to see situations and people from His perspective.

2. Pray that His Kingdom will come on this earth and all that He has planned and purposed for us will be done as it has been done in heaven. All that we need here on this earth is already waiting for us to call it down from heaven. The reason we should desire to see God's Kingdom come on this earth is because, without His Kingdom on this earth, we would be in a hopeless state with sin running rampant.

3. Ask God to fill you and His people with His Word and Spirit (daily bread). We need the outpouring

and overflowing of His Spirit and Word in our lives so that we will be the light in the dark world and be equipped for living our lives as He desires.

4.    Ask the Lord to forgive you of your sins as you have forgiven those who have sinned against you. God promises in 1 John 1:9 that He will forgive if we confess.

5.    Ask for His divine strength to be at work in you so when you are tempted, you won't fall into sin's trap. Ask for His awesome power to crush Satan's plans to tempt you by using the Word of God.

Conclude each prayer in Jesus' name. As your understanding of the Bible increases, you will be able to teach others (saved and unsaved alike) the biblical truths that have transformed your walk with the Lord.

## Tell Others About Christ

I remember when I was petrified to tell others about Jesus Christ. In fact, I made every excuse in the book *not* to tell others about Him. I would randomly speak about Jesus Christ at times but was never brave enough to share the truth of the Gospel with a stranger or friend. As an introvert, I was not at all comfortable talking or sharing my ideas, thoughts, or feelings with anyone. However, when I gave my heart back to the Lord, I—like Mary Magdalene, the Apostle Paul, and John— realized that I have been forgiven of all my sins and had everything to lose if I lost Jesus. When I realized that I have been loved deeply, I was moved by God's love to share my faith and boldly present the message of hope to others. I found that my desire to see others come to Christ was far greater than my fear to share my faith.

As Christians, we have been commissioned by Jesus to "Go therefore and make disciples of all the nations, baptizing them in the name of the Father and of the Son and of the Holy Spirit" (Matthew 28:19). We are to present the Gospel, the Message of Hope, to all we encounter. Why? We were commissioned to do this by Christ because our lives have been changed by His saving grace. Think about it: what better person is there to present to the world that Jesus loves them and died for their sins than one whose life has been changed by that exact message of hope?

> **1 Corinthians 5:18-21** — *Now all things are of God, who has reconciled us to Himself through Jesus Christ, and has given us the ministry of reconciliation, that is, that God was in Christ reconciling the world to Himself, not imputing their trespasses to them, and has committed to us the word of reconciliation. Now then, we are ambassadors for Christ, as though God were pleading through us: we implore you on Christ's behalf, be reconciled to God. For He made Him who knew no sin to be sin for us, that we might become the righteousness of God in Him.*

Since we are the righteousness of God in Jesus Christ (we are in right standing with God because of Jesus Christ), we have an obligation and the wonderful honor of sharing our faith in Christ with those who need it the most. As Paul has written in 1 Corinthians, all Christians have been given the ministry of reconciliation. That is, all Christians has been given the responsibility to tell others that God desires to be reconciled to them again through faith in Christ. We are ambassadors *for* Christ. Therefore, we ought to finish the work (of telling the world about God's love and salvation) that "Jesus began both to do and teach, until the day in which He was taken up" (Acts 1:1-2). Whether it's family members, friends, colleagues, or strangers, we should be compelled by the love of Christ to tell the dying world that there is a cure for their sinful condition!

Imagine how much better the world would be if "Thy kingdom come, Thy will be done in earth, as it is in heaven" (Matthew 6:10, KJV). Therefore, we who hold the truth should not keep it a secret from the rest of the world. God is not just our personal God; He is the I AM! He is God over all the earth! Like a city on the *hill cannot be hidden*, our faith should not be kept a secret from the people who need to hear it the most!

> **Romans 1:16** – *For I am not ashamed of the gospel of Christ, for it is the power of God to salvation for everyone who believes, for the Jew first and also for the Greek.*

When necessary, I like to share my personal struggles with others to highlight the power and mercies of God. I humbly consider myself just blessed to know Jesus Christ for myself. I do not wish to be more than who God created me to be. I am content to serve Him and being loved by Him is more than enough for me. I never imagined I would have to overcome so much dissention in my family, personal mental struggles, addiction, and other strongholds in my life. I never imagined writing a book to help others in their walk with the Lord. I am too deeply moved by the love God has for me and the changes He has brought in my life to keep anything He has accomplished a secret. I encourage you to make a daily effort to tell others what God has done for you!

# 7

## CHALLENGES
## AS A CHRISTIAN

To be candid, as a believer who has been saved for quite a few years, I can say with much certainty that anyone who believes on Jesus Christ will face challenges. These challenges will vary in type and degree and will pertain to both faith and the individual. Some challenges include doubt, worry, family issues, identity, temptations, and social pressures. However, the most common challenge that every Christian will face is persecution.

> **2 Timothy 3:12** – *Yes, and all who desire to live godly in Christ Jesus will suffer persecution.*

## Persecution Against the Christian Faith

We are faced with challenges because we live in a fallen (sinful) world, and we cannot escape it because "the whole world lies under the sway of the wicked one" (1 John 5:19). However, as believers, we must deal with these trials as well as the challenges that come with being a Christian. Therefore, believers should not be surprised if they face ridicule, bodily harm, hostility, or any other ill treatment because of their faith in Christ. For Jesus tells us, "If the world hate you, ye know that it hated me before it hated you. If ye were of the world, the world would love his own: but because ye are not of the world, but I have chosen you out of the world, therefore the world hateth you. Remember the word that I said unto you, The servant is not greater than his lord. If they have persecuted me, they will also persecute you; if they have kept my saying, they will keep yours also" (John 15:18-20, KJV).

The world will hate Christians because the world hated Christ. However, despite certain persecution, we are left with these comforting words from our Lord Jesus Christ:

**John 16:33, KJV** – *These things I have spoken unto you, that in me ye might have peace. In the world ye shall have tribulation: but be of good cheer; I have overcome the world.*

And the Apostle John tells us that "this is the victory that has overcome the world—our faith" (1 John 5:4). We have the assurance as believers that we need not fear any opposition or persecution, because our faith in Jesus Christ causes us to overcome and triumph over the devil and anything (or anyone) he uses against us.

## How a Christian Responds to Persecution

As believers, our response to persecution should be to love and rejoice. The following passages of scriptures depict the rejoicing attitude that every believer should have in response to persecution:

> **2 Corinthian 2:10** (*emphasis added*) – *Therefore,* ***I take pleasure*** *in infirmities, in reproaches, in needs, in persecutions, in distresses, for Christ's sake. For when I am weak, then I am strong.*

> **1 Peter 4:13** (*emphasis* added) – *But* ***rejoice*** *to the extent that you partake of Christ's sufferings, that when His glory is revealed, you may also* ***be glad about exceeding joy.***

> **2 Corinthians 12:9** (emphasis added) – *And He said to me, 'My grace is sufficient for you, for My strength is made perfect in weakness.' Therefore, most* ***gladly I will rather boast*** *in my infirmities, that the power of Christ may rest upon me.*

We ought to rejoice when we suffer for Christ's sake, because persecution is a sign that the believer is aligned with God's will and counted worthy to suffer for His name. When facing various trials for our faith, we should take exceeding comfort that we are suffering just as our beloved Savior did. Therefore, instead of seeking revenge on our offenders, we should follow Christ's command to "*love* your enemies, *bless* those who curse you, *do good* to those who hate you, and *pray* for those who spitefully use you and persecute you" (Matthew 5:44, emphasis added).

In 2017, a friend and I faced constant ridicule, opposition, slander, name-calling, bodily harm, and isolation because of our faith in Jesus Christ. I recall nights at our workplace when we had to encourage each other in the Lord just to make it to our next break. In fact, we sought the Lord for guidance and strength at every opportunity we were afforded, because the persecution escalated beyond description. I always took comfort in knowing that all these things occurred because I walked with Jesus. However, there were times when I was not sure if I could keep loving, blessing, doing good, and praying for my enemies.

> **2 Corinthians 2:14, KJV** – *Now thanks be unto God, which always causeth us to triumph in Christ, and maketh manifest the savour of his knowledge by us in every place.*

It was only by the grace and strength of God that I overcame one of the most difficult times of my life. I remember praying during those days that God would use my pain for His glory and rejoicing because I was counted worthy to suffer for His wonderful name. Instead of my natural tendency to retaliate, I focused much more on the example Christ left for us: "Who, when He was reviled, did not revile in return; when He suffered, He did not threaten, but committed Himself to Him who judges righteously" (1 Peter 2:23).

When I was a younger Christian, I went through a time when I was forced into isolation from all who claimed to be my friends. When I rededicated my life to the Lord, all my friends basically abandoned me. My father still was not the nicest to me after my rededication. As I said prior, my self-esteem suffered greatly at his hands. Even after rededicating my life back to God, I was faced with comments against my character, but this time, it was about *how* I was serving the Lord. In my father's eyes, everything I was doing and what God was revealing to me was not important in comparison to His walk with the Lord. I was comforted in knowing that God saw me much different than how my father saw me.

During both instances, God's love for me compelled me to pray for those who mistreated me. In every case of suffering, I consider what I have done to God. I ridiculed God, abandoned Him, and did wrong to the point that He had to die for my sin! "Blessed are you when men hate you, and when they exclude you, and revile you and cast out your name as evil, for the Son of Man's sake. Rejoice in that day and leap for joy! For indeed your reward is great in heaven, for in like manner their fathers did to the prophets" (Luke 6:22-23).

Time will fail me to list all the ways we will suffer as Christians (i.e., through family members and dynamics, job-related issues, etc.). There are undoubtedly many challenges that each believer must face but be comforted in knowing that "the battle is not yours, but God's" (2 Chronicles 20:15 KJV). God has you safely in His hands and will not allow you to face something you are not able to conquer. Remember, "We are more than conquerors through Him that loved us." (Romans 8:37, KJV).

# 8

## EXHORTATION

To all believers in Christ Jesus, it is my heart's desire to see all my brothers and sisters in Christ live their lives fully in the richness of His grace and the limitlessness of His love. I am passionate to see the sinner come to repentance, the new believer growing in the knowledge of God, and the mature believer remaining steadfast in the faith. I hope all will continue to walk worthy of Christ and not allow worldly distractions, people, or situations to keep you from experiencing all that God has for your life. From a sincere heart, I love you and pray that our God will continuously keep you as the Good Shepherd He is!

I encourage you to love one another as Christ Jesus loves us and know and understand the importance of serving Him. I encourage you to read the Bible daily and make it your priority to draw near to God so He will draw near to you. It is our duty as Christians to fear God and keep His commandments and teach others to do the same.

May our Lord God bless you in all your ways and may you grow daily in His likeness so that your light will shine brightly in this dark world.

# ABOUT THE AUTHOR

Nakia Trader was born and raised in Dover, Delaware. Since the age of 11, she has written dozens of songs, poems, and short stories that have been showcased in her home church, other churches, and school.

She has traveled to various states across the country as well as internationally doing missionary work and assisting individuals in growing closer to the Lord. She decided to postpone her missionary work to concentrate on her educational goals. She has since obtained degrees in human services and psychology.

Nakia resumed her passion in doing the Lord's work by becoming the cofounder of Way of Truth Evangelistic Ministries and implementing outreach programs such as Beautiful Feet Evangelism and All or Nothing: Provisions. This latter ministry is done with ministry partner and friend, Valyncia, focusing on giving the Gospel and provisions to those in need in our community.

Regardless of her accomplishments, Nakia's greatest passion and desire is to reach lost souls for the Kingdom of God by declaring the Gospel throughout the nations and helping disciple new believers in a closer relationship with God.

If you want to connect with Nakia and explore her video and literary work, visit her on Facebook page:

- facebook.com/nakianatrader89/
- facebook.com/nogimmicksjustTruth/
- or on Twitter@ktraderGC98

Made in the USA
Middletown, DE
28 September 2022

11010253R00047